DISCOVERING
Church Life

24 KEYS TO BUILDING COMMUNITY

FRANK DAMAZIO

STUDENT EDITION

Published by
City Christian Publishing
9200 NE Fremont
Portland, OR. 97213

Discovering Church Life
24 Keys to Building Community
Student Edition

ISBN 10-Digit: 1-59383-040-8
ISBN 13-Digit: 978-1-59383-040-3

© Copyright 2007 by Frank Damazio

City Christian Publishing is a ministry of City Bible Church and is dedicated to serving the local church and its leaders through the production and distribution of quality equipping resources. It is our prayer that these materials, proven in the context of the local church, will equip leaders in exalting the Lord and extending the kingdom.

For a free catalog of additional resources from City Christian Publishing, please call 1-800-777-6057 or visit our web site at www.CityChristianPublishing.com.

All Scripture quotations, unless otherwise indicated, are taken from the *New King James* version. Copyright 1979,1980,1982 by Thomas Nelson, Inc. Publishers. Used by permission. All rights reserved.

All rights reserved. No portion of this book may be reproduced, stored in a retrieval system, or transmitted in any form or by any means electronic, mechanical, photocopy, facsimile, recording, or any except for brief quotations in printed reviews without the prior permission of the Publisher.

First Edition, July 2007
Printed in the United States of America

DISCOVERING CHURCH LIFE
Table of Contents

Solid Foundation

Introduction

We are not original in placing great importance upon the teaching on foundations. We have scriptural precedent. The Lord Jesus Christ and the Apostles put great emphasis on this subject. Without proper foundations, the rest of the structure will be threatened, endangered with delayed disaster. The building is no stronger than the foundation. The burden of this lesson will be instruction on the proper way of laying a biblical foundation. Since the foundation bears the weight of the entire structure, it must be done well. The taller the building the deeper the foundation. Let us dig deep and lay the foundation upon a solid rock so as to build a strong structure.

I. The Importance of Proper Foundations

A. Definition of *"foundation"*

1. Greek, *"something put down, to lay a basis for something to be erected"*

2. English, *"ground work on which something is laid, or built; that which is built on foundation is only as strong as the ground work"*

B. Foundations — the Determining Factor *(1 Cor 3:9-13)*

1. Determine the stability of the building

2. Determine the strength of the building when under storms *(Mt 7:24-27)*

3. Determine the structure of the building *(Heb 6:3)*

C. OT examples of proper foundations

1. _____ *Ex 26:15-19*

2. _____ *Gn 22; 2 Chr 4-5; Ps 87:1*

3. _____ *Ez 3:6-12, 5:16; 6:3; Hg 2:18; Zec 4:9; 8:9; 12:1*

II. Preparation for Laying Proper Foundations

    A. Preparation of examination — *Lk 6:48-49*

    B. Attitude of carefulness — *1 Cor 3:9-13*

III. Laying a Proper Foundation

    A. Principle of obedience

        1. _____ *Mt 7:24-27; Jas 1:22-25*

        2. _____ *Mt 23:3; 7:21*

        3. _____ *Heb 2:1-2; 3:15-16; Mt 13:13; Lk 8:8; Jn 15:14*

    B. Principle of Biblical conviction

Questions

    1. How much importance does God place upon foundations? (Illustrate)

    2. What should be the attitude of the one laying the foundation?

    3. What guarantees the foundation to be solid and able to stand the storms?

    4. Explain in your own words the "digging deep" process in your personal experience while preparing for laying your foundation.

Memory Verse:

Matthew 7:24-27

Proper Christian Birth

Introduction

Whenever a child is born today, it is given a birth certificate. This certificate validates the time, proper name and description of the infant. As in the natural, so in the spiritual. Christians today need to examine their birth certificates. Have they had a proper Christian birth? This lesson will examine the need, process and evidence of a true Christian birth.

I. The Need To Be Born Again

A. _____ *Rom 5:12-19; 3:23; I Pt 2:23*

B. _____ *Mt 24:12; 2 Tm 3:1-5*

II. The Variety of Terms Used To Describe Salvation

A. _____ *"to change the condition, nature and character of something"*

B. _____ *"remission of sin, guilt and punishment, act by which a sinner is freed through faith from the penalty of son and is accepted by God as righteous and worthy of being saved"*

C. _____ *"to change or turn into something different"*

D. _____ *"to form or bring into existence again, a spiritual renewal"*

E. _____ *"whenever men by their own fault or through some superior power have come under the control of someone else and have lost their freedom, they need a third party to fulfill the work of redemption"*

F. _____ *"to restore to original state, complete healing or relationships, bringing two parties together who were at enmity"*

G. _____ *"to deliver from, to heal so as to make whole"*

III. The Process of New Birth

A. The term "born again" is used more in the Johannine writings than in any other book. The Apostle John delivers to us the true New Testament theology on being born again. This term is used 10 times in the Gospel of John and 6 times in John's Epistles.

B. Natural birth compared to spiritual birth — *1 Cor 15:45-46; Jn 3:1-13.*

1. _____   1. _____

2. _____   2. _____

3. _____   3. _____

4. _____   4. _____

5. _____   5. _____

C. Examining repentance.

1. Repentance: Greek, *metanoieo* —*"to think differently, to care or regret, reversal of actions"*

2 Repentance is not conviction of sin, worldly sorrow, believism or pleasing others by your changing.

3. Repentance must touch your mind, will and emotions. *Lk 15:18-20*

4. Repentance must bear fruit in the Believer's life.

IV. The Evidence of Being Born Again

Matthew 3:8; John 8:33-59

A. The evidence of _____. *Jn 8:41; 1 Jn 2:29*

B. The evidence of _____ in your heart expressed in worship and works. *Jn 8:42*

C. The evidence of _____ in the Word of God. *Jn 8:43, 47; Lk 24:31, 32, 45*

D. The evidence of _____ of God. *1 Pt 2:2*

E. The evidence of not continuing in _____ *Prv 28:13; 1 Jn 3:9; 5:18*

F. The evidence of a _____ for yourself, others and even your enemies. *1 Jn 4:7, 8, 11, 12; 3:16*

G. The evidence of _____ of Christ. *1 Jn 5:1-3*

H. The evidence of a desire and a God-given strength to _____ *1 Jn 5:4*

Questions:

1. Explain in your own words the interpretation of *Romans 5:12.*

2. What are the four steps involved in being born again?

3. How does a person know for sure they have been born again?

4. Share in your own words the experiences of new birth in your life.

Memory Verse:

1 John 5:4, 18

The Doctrine of Baptisms

I. Different Baptisms in the New Testament — Hebrews 6:2

A. _____ *Mt 3:11*

B. _____ *Mt 3:13-17*

C. _____ *Lk 12:50*

D. _____ *Acts 2:38; Mt 28:18-20*

E. _____ *Acts 11:16*

II. The Doctrine of Water Baptism

A. Definition of the word *"baptize, baptism"*

    1. Greek root-word, *bapto* — *"to dip something into a fluid and then take it out; to cover with a fluid." Lk 16:24; Jn 13:26; Rev 19:13*

    2. Greek, *baptizo* — *"to cause something to be dipped; to be plunged; submerged into." 2 Kgs 5:14*

B. Old Testament baptisms (typical of the New Testament believer's baptism)

    1. _____ *1 Cor 10:1-5; Ex 13-14*

    2. _____ *Ex 29:4; Lv 8:6*

    3. _____ *Gn 1:7-11*

    4. _____ *Gn 8 and 9*

    5. _____ *Lv 14:1-9*

    6. _____ *Nm 19*

C. New Testament example of Water Baptism

   1. The Gospels —

     (a) Jesus, the Son of God, was immersed totally in water baptism. Mt 3

     (b) Jesus commands the Apostles to teach water baptism. Mk 16:15-18

   2. The Book of Acts —

     (a) The Church at Jerusalem — Acts 2:36-40

     (b) The Church at Samaria — Acts 8:12-38

     (c) The Church at Damascus — Acts 9:5-18

     (d) The Church at Caesarea — Acts 10:48

     (e) The Church at Philippi — Acts 16:14-34

     (f) The Church at Corinth — Acts 18:8

     (g) The Church at Ephesus — Acts 19:1-6

D. New Testament teaching on Water Baptism

   1. _____ *Acts 2:37-38*

   2. _____ *Ro 6:3-10; Gen 8 and 9*

   3. _____ *Ro 6:3-6*

   4. _____ *Mt 28:18-20; Acts 2:37-40*

   5. _____ *Col 2:12*

   6. _____ *Gal 3:27*

   7. _____ *Col 2:11-12*

III. The Doctrine of Baptism in the Holy Spirit

A. The Holy Spirit foretold and foreshadowed in the Old Testament

   1. The Holy Spirit rested upon a select few in the Old Testament, enabling them for specific jobs (prophets, priests, kings and judges).

2. The Holy Spirit baptism was foretold by Old Testament prophets. *Is 28:11-12; Ez 11:19-20; 37:14; Jl 2:28-30*

3. The Holy Spirit was foreshadowed by Old Testament types. *Ex 19:18-20, Lev 14:8-18, 1 Cor 10:1-2*

B. Holy Spirit baptism promised in the Gospels

1. By John the Baptist — *Mt 3:11*

2. By the Lord Jesus Christ — *Jn 1:33; 7:38-39; Acts 1:4, 8*

C. Holy Spirit baptism in the Book of Acts (evidence of baptism)

1. Jerusalem *(Acts 2:1-13)* _____

2. Samaria *(Acts 8:14-17)* _____

3. House of Cornelius *(Acts 10:44-48)* _____

4. Ephesus *(Acts 19:1-6)* _____

5. Paul *(Acts 9:17-18; 1 Cor 14:18)* _____

D. Variety of Biblical terms describing this experience

1. _____ The truth here is that the Believer must be totally immersed, submerged and saturated with the Holy Spirit. *Mt 3:11; Acts 1:5; 1 Cor 12:13; Heb 6:2*

2. _____ The truth of filling views the Believer as the vessel or container for the Spirit of God. There may be one baptism but many fillings. *Acts 2:4; 4:8, 31; 6:3-5; 9:17; 13:9*

3. _____ The truth emphasized here is the Holy Spirit as a liquid that is freely given. *Acts 2:17; 10:45; Jl 2:28-29*

4. _____ The analogy here seems to be of rain that comes from above to bring refreshing and fruitfulness. *Acts 8:16; 10:44; 11:15; 19:6; Lk 24:49; Jn 15:26*

5. _____ The truth brought forth here is that this experience of baptism in the Holy Spirit involves being clothed with the power of God. *Lk 24:49; Acts 1:8; 4:33; 10:38; 1 Thes 1:5*

6. _____ This term signifies the Holy Spirit coming to the Believer as a stamp with a signet or private mark for security, preservation, genuineness or authenticity. *Jn 6:27; 2 Cor 1:21-22*

7. _____ The term "earnest" speaks of a pledge or a foretaste of something to come. *2 Cor 1:22; 5:5; Heb 6:4-5*

E. How to receive the Baptism of the Holy Spirit

1. Must be born again — *Acts 2:38-39*

2. Must recognize the Holy Spirit is given as a gift — *Lk 11:13; Acts 2:38; 10:45; 11:17*

3. Must desire and ask for this gift — *Acts 19:2, 6; Lk 11:9-13 (Amp)*

4. Must receive the Holy Spirit, in an act of hunger, willingness and faith — *Acts 2:38; 8:15-19; 10:47; 19:2; Jn 20:22*

Questions:

1. What do the Old Testament types of water baptism teach us about Christian baptism?

2. Explain in your own words the reason Jesus was baptized in water.

3. What is the evidence of being filled with the Holy Spirit? How do we know this?

4. What must a person do to be baptized in the Holy Spirit?

Memory Verse:

Acts 2:38-39

Matthew 3:11

Born Into the Kingdom

John 3:1-5, Matthew 16:16-18

Introduction

The Believer must understand the distinction between the Church and the Kingdom. How do you become part of the Church? How are you brought into the Kingdom? Through the study of Scripture, we find that the Believer is born into the kingdom, but he is *added* to the *Church*. In this lesson, we will study the nature, scope and government of the Kingdom of God and how we as Believers relate to this Kingdom.

I. The Definition of the Word "Kingdom"

A. Greek, *basileia* — *"a king's domain; the fact of being king by his power and position; status of the king is shown by the area over which he reigns, or governs as having total control; the rule of the king in the lives of willing subjects"*

B. English, *"the word 'kingdom' is taken from two Old English words; the word 'king' refers to the ruler in authority, and the word 'dom' speaks of the king's jurisdiction, his realm or domain"*

C. Application — when we speak of the Kingdom of God, we are speaking of the rule and government of the Lord Jesus Christ upon my life, that is evidenced by a continual obedience to the spiritual laws of this kingdom.

II. The Scope of the Kingdom of God

III. The New Testament Message—The Kingdom

A. _____ Mt 3:2 *"Repent for the kingdom of heaven is at hand"*

B. _____ Mt 4:17 *"Repent for the kingdom of heaven is at hand"*

C. _____ Mt 10:7 *"Repent for the kingdom of heaven is at hand"*

D. _____ Mt 24:14 *"The gospel of the kingdom shall be preached"*

E. _____ Acts 1:3 *"Teaching things pertaining to the kingdom of God."*

F. _____ Acts 8:12 *"Preaching the kingdom of God"*
14:22; 19:8; 20:25; 28:31

G. _____ Rom 14:17; 1 Cor 4:20; 6:9; Gal 5:21; Eph 5:5; Col 1:13;
1 Thes 2:12; Heb 1:8

IV. Biblical Concepts of the Kingdom of God

A. The Kingdom of God is an _____ Ps 145:10-13

B. The Kingdom of God is _____ Lk 17:21

C. The Kingdom of God is an _____ 1 Cor 4:20

D. The Kingdom of God is an _____ Heb 12:28

E. The Kingdom of God is _____ Rom 14:17

V. Entering the Kingdom of God

A. Embracing the name JESUS _____
Mt 1:16; 18, 21

B. Embracing the name CHRIST _____
Mt 11:2; 16:12, 20; 23:8-10; 24:5; 26:63, 68

C. Embracing the name LORD _____
Acts 9:5-17, 27, 29, 31, 35, 42; Rom 10:9-13; Phil 2:11; Rev 4:8; 17:14

VI. The Laws of the Kingdom

A. We are living in a generation of lawlessness.

   1. Lawless:— Greek, *"not subject to the law, violator of the law."* 1 Tm 1:9

   2. *"Anomia"* is translated in our English Bible as these words:

      - *transgressor (Mk 15:28)*
      - *wicked (Acts 2:23)*
      - *without law (1 Cor 9:21)*
      - *unlawful deeds (2 Pt 2:8)*
      - *iniquity (Mt 7:23; 13:41; 23:28; Rom 6:19; 2 Cor 6:14)*

B. We are to be an example of righteousness of the law.

   1. *Rom 8:4; 13:10*
   2. *Heb 8:10; 10:16*
   3. *Pss 1:2; 37:31; 40:8; 119:97*
   4. *Is 42:21*
   5. *Lk 1:6*

Questions:

1. What is the difference between the Church and the Kingdom?
2. Explain in your own words how a person enters the Kingdom of God.
3. Share your personal experience of embracing the name of the Lord Jesus Christ.
4. What are the laws of the Kingdom of God?

Memory Verse:

Romans 14:17

Added to the Church

Introduction

In the previous lesson, we have discussed the experience of being born again. The proper Christian birth has profound ramifications upon every area of our Christian walk. In the last lesson, we found that we were *"born into the Kingdom."* Birth into the Kingdom of God is one aspect of what happens to a new Christian upon receiving Jesus as both Christ and Lord. After birth into the Kingdom comes this next step for the new Believer; he must be *added to a local Body.* In the natural, we do not expect a new born baby to be left on the streets or in a park somewhere, but he is born into a *family.* This birth brings joy to the family along with many adjustments and new-found responsibilities.

I. The Pattern of the New Testament Church

    A. _____

       Greek, *"to put into, to be joined unto, to gather with any company of people"*

       1. *Acts 2:41*

       2. *Acts 2:47*

       3. *Acts 5:13-14*

       4. *Acts 11:22-26*

    B. _____

       Greek, *"to put or place, to set or establish, fix in a certain place"*

       1. *1 Cor 12:18, 28*

       2. *Acts 20:28*

       3. *1 Tm 1:12, 2:7*

       4. *2 Tm 1:11*

       5. *Ps 68:6*

C. _____

Greek, *"to be put into a place of rest, a special habitation, to cause to rest so as to lay down"*

1. *Jn 14:2-3*

2. *Eph 4:11-12*

3. *Prv 27:8*

4. *Eccl 10:4*

II. The Balance of One Body But Many Members

A. Illustration

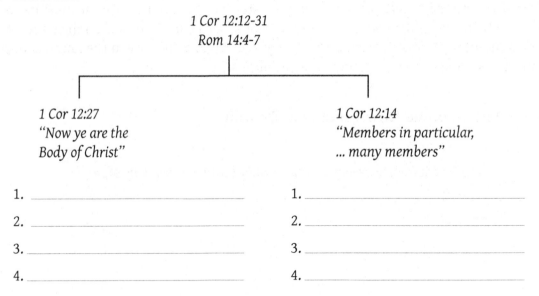

1 Cor 12:12-31
Rom 14:4-7

1 Cor 12:27
"Now ye are the Body of Christ"

1. _____

2. _____

3. _____

4. _____

1 Cor 12:14
"Members in particular, ... many members"

1. _____

2. _____

3. _____

4. _____

B. Accepting God's placement in the Body

1. *1 Cor 12:11, 18* — God sets members in as it pleases Him

2. *Rom 12:3-4* — We are to think soberly of ourselves
    ... recognize our limitations
    ... recognize our placement
    ... recognize our measure of grace

III. The Responsibilities of Being Set into a Local Body

A. Responsible to _____ each member of the Body

    1. *1 Cor 12:25*

    2. *Heb 13:17*

    3. *Ez 33:2-7*

    4. *Gn 4:9*

B. Responsible to _____ members of the Body

    1. *Gal 6:2*

    2. *Ru 4:15*

    3. *Is 58:12*

    4. *Ps 23:3*

C. Responsible to _____ members of the Body

    1. *Heb 3:13*

    2. *Heb 10:24*

D. Responsible to _____ life and strength to members of the Body

    1. *2 Cor 8:14*

    2. *Phil 2:30*

E. Responsible to _____ all members of the Body

    1. *1 Cor 14:3-5, 12*

    2. *Rom 14:1-3, 7-8, 12-21*

    3. *Eph 4:12, 15, 16*

F. Responsible to _____ to the leadership of the Body

    1. *Heb 13:7, 17*

    2. *1 Pt 5:5*

    3. *Eph 5:21*

Questions:

1. After a person is born again, what is the next biblical step?

2. Who sets members into the Body, and for what purpose? Refer to I Cor 12:18, 28.

3. How does a person practically fulfill Romans 12:3?

4. Where has God placed you? What specific local Body? What is your specific contribution to the local Body?

Memory Verse:

Psalm 68:6

John 3:1-5

Matthew 16:16-18

Corporate Gatherings

Introduction

We are not converted to live our Christian life alone. We are to be *"builded together"* in Christ, being placed into His universal Church by being joined to a local Church. When we come into a living relationship with Christ, we also should come into a whole new way of living in association with one another. Many Christians make a basic mistake when they reject the opportunity to be involved in a corporate gathering of God's people. This common rejection among some Christians results in a life-long spiritual immaturity.

I. The Two-Fold Aspect of the Church

    A. The _____ — Mt 16:13-19

    B. The _____ — Mt 18:16-18

        1. 90 percent of Scriptures on the Church speak of the local Church.

        2. Most all of the New Testament Epistles are written to local Churches.

II. The Importance of the Local Gatherings of God's People

    A. The fact of the local gathering

        1. _____ *"when ye are gathered together"*

        2. _____ *"when ye come together into one place"*

        3. _____ *"when ye come together to eat"*

        4. _____ *"yet in the Church"*

        5. _____ *"the whole Church be come together in one place"*

        6. _____ *"how is it then brethren? When ye come together every one of you..."*

7. _____ *"and all that believed were together"*

8. _____ *"and when they had prayed, the place was shaken"*

9. _____ *"and many were gathered together praying"*

B. Local gathering not to be neglected

1. *Hebrews 10:25* (Amplified) *"Not forsaking or neglecting to assemble together as Believers, as is the habit of some people, but admonishing, warning, urging and encouraging one another, and all the more faithfully as you see the day approaching..."*

2. Common excuses —

   (a) *"We can get just as much from God alone in our bedroom as we can in a local Church gathering."*

   (b) *"It's not where we meet with God, but how we meet."*

   (c) *"Our family is so busy with many activities that there are just not enough hours in the week to attend Church."*

III. The Purpose of the Local Gathering of God's People

A. To receive the ministry of the _____
   Eph 4:11-13

B. To receive _____ from the Holy Spirit through the many-membered Body of Christ. *1 Cor 14:3-4, 12, 19, 26*

C. To become _____ and _____ place of refuge for all who seek help.

D. To become a _____ of the Church in every given locality for

   the purpose of _____ for righteousness.

Questions:

1. What is the difference between *Matthew 16:18* and *Matthew 18:16-17,* concerning the Church?

2. What are some of the common obstacles that keep people from coming together with God's people?

3. Why does Satan try so hard to keep people from coming together?

4. When the Local Church comes together, what do you contribute to that gathering?

Memory Verse

1 Corinthians 14:26

Home Gatherings

Introduction

In the New Testament, we see Christ ministering both in the synagogue and in homes. In the Book of Acts, we see the Early Church meeting in the Temple and house to house. This pattern is given to us by the New Testament Local Church found in the Book of Acts. The Home Fellowship Meetings are not to be a substitute for the corporate meetings, but a supplement to them. Everyone has a distinctive need to be loved, accepted and to feel needed, and the Home Fellowship Meetings are designed to meet these personal needs.

I. The Two-Fold Aspect of Salvation

A. *Acts 2:37-47 v. 40 "and with many other words did he testify and exhort, saying save yourself from this untoward generation."*

B. Two-fold aspect of salvation

"God saves us"
from death and hell

Jn 3:16-16
Eph 2:5, 8
Lk 7:50
Acts 2:21, 47

"We save ourselves"
from this present
evil generation

Acts 2:40
Phil 2:12
1 Tm 4:16
Jas 1:21

C. Save yourself by obedience to the New Testament pattern — *Acts 2:42-47.*

    1. Continue steadfastly in _____

    2. Continue steadfastly in _____

    3. Continue steadfastly in _____

    4. Continue steadfastly in _____

II. Continuing Steadfastly in Fellowship

A. The definition of the word "fellowship"

    1. English, *"the condition of being an associate, mutual association of persons on equal friendly terms, a mutual sharing of experience, activity, interest or partnership"*

    2. Greek, *koinonia* — *"to share what one has with another, so that both can prosper; the word expresses inner relationship, participation and impartation"*

    3. Translated in the New Testament as communicate, communion, distribution, contribution, fellowship.

B. Examples of the word *"fellowship"*

    1. In the Godhead — fellowship between the Father, Son and Holy Spirit

    2. In the creation and relationship of Adam and Eve — *Gn 1:26, 2:1-25*

Adam   *Eve*

*Gn 2:25
need for:*

    (a) _____

    (b) _____

    (c) _____

    (d) _____

    (e) _____

(f) _____

(g) _____

III. The Balance of the New Testament Local Church

A. Balance of Temple gatherings and Home gatherings

B. Home Fellowship Ministry is likened unto the cells of the human body.

TEMPLE	HOUSE
Usually the emphasis is on teaching, instruction, feeding, prophetic song and Word.	Usually the emphasis is on sharing, relationships, encouragement, prayer, and Body sharing.
Eph 4:11-12	*Rom 12:1-10, I Cor 12:27, Eph 4:16*
1. *Acts 2:46*	1. *Acts 2:46*
2. *Acts 3:1*	2. *Acts 5:42*
3. *Acts 5:20-21*	3. *Acts 8:3*
4. *Acts 5:25*	4. *Acts 12:12-17*
5. *Acts 5:42*	5. *Acts 16:14-15, 31, 34, 40*
6. *Heb 10:25*	6. *Acts 17:1-5*
	7. *Acts 18:7-8*
	8. *Acts 20:20; 21:8-12*
	9. *Rom 16:5; I Cor 16:19*

1. Each biological cell moves, grows, reacts, protects, reproduces a tiny miniature of the larger body, and contributes to the life of the body.

2. Each cell is different; a diversity of shapes and sizes.

3. Each cell has a sense of order, a sense of loyalty and responsibility to a higher leadership.

4. Each cell depends on community life for survival with a continual contribution to other cells.

5. Each cell has the capacity to grow, reproduce itself, divide into two other cells; multiplication by division.

6. Each cell has antibodies to fight assaults of enemy viruses.

7. Each cell has the potential for rebellion that breaks the laws of the body, damages the body, and becomes a cancer cell.

Questions:

1. What is our responsibility in saving ourselves from this untoward generation?

2. What hinders us from sharing our life with others in the Body?

3. Which part of this lesson has specifically spoken to your heart?

4. What steps can be taken to put this teaching into practice?

Memory Verse

Acts 2:46-47

Doctrine of Covering

Introduction

The Bible speaks of the last days as being a time of a great outpouring of the Holy Spirit and a time of great spiritual deception of the devil. We can witness to both of these facts by the events transpiring in the 20th Century. In the midst of all the trouble and pressure, the Lord has promised a city of refuge for those who would run into it. The truth of covering for God's people is of great importance to those who will stand in these last days.

I. The Definition of the Word "Covering"

A. There are eleven different Hebrew words used which are translated *"covering."* These eleven words are very close in meaning, and can be summed up in two major aspects:

   1. *"a blotting out."* Man needs a covering of blood to blot out sin in his life.

   2. *"a protective covering."* man needs a protective covering over his life from the enemy.

B. The Hebrew also brings out the thought of *"making a hedge or a fence in order to protect and guard that which is valued and loved."*

II. The Need for Covering

A. We are living in a time of _____.

   1. *Dn 12:1; Zec 1:15*
   2. *Pss 9:9; 46:1; 59:16; 27:4-6; 32:7*
   3. *2 Cor 4:8*

B. We are living in a time of _____.

   1. *Pss 55:8; 107:28-29*
   2. *Mt 7:24-27; 14:22-24*

3. Three types of storms:
   - *we bring them on ourselves*
   - *God brings them*
   - *Satan brings them*

C. We are living in a time of _____
   1. *Mt 24:4-6; Mk 13:22*
   2. *Ti 1:10, 2 Tm 3:13; 1 Tm 4:1*
   3. *2 Thes 2:10-12*
   4. *Eph 5:6-7; Gal 6:7*

III. The Truth of Covering

A. Covering in the Old Testament
   1. _____ *Ex 26:14; 35:11-12; 36:19, 39:34; Nm 9:15-16*
   2. _____ *Ex 37:9; 25:20*
   3. _____ *Nm 4:20; 19:15*
   4. _____ *Ex 28:42*
   5. _____ *Is 51:16; 61:10; Ex 33:12; Pss 91:4; 104:7*

B. Covering in the New Testament
   1. _____ *1 Cor 11:3; Eph 5:21-25*
   2. _____ *Eph 4:11-13; Heb 13:7, 17*

IV. The Doctrine of Covering Illustrated

A. The woman in the Garden of Eden — *1 Cor 11:10; Gn 3:1-15; Pss 34:7; 91:1-4, 9-11; Mt 18:10*

B. The Passover celebration — *Ex 12:3-30*

C. The cities of refuge — *Nm 35:11-26; Heb 6:18; Jos 20:2, 9; Dt 19:3*

V. Attitudes to be Warned Against

A. The attitude of _____. *Prv 6:17; Mt 7:22; 1 Jn 2:16*

B. The attitude of _____. *Prv 14:15*

C. The attitude of _____. *Prv 3:5; 28:26*

D. The attitude of _____. *Dt 15:7; Jn 12:40; Col 3:19; Mk 7:6*

E. The attitude of _____. *1 Sm 15:23; Pss 66:7, 68:6; Jer 5:23*

F. The attitude of _____. *Rom 1:18-32; 2 Sm 11:1-17*

Questions:

1. Explain and define the word "covering" in your own words.

2. Why do you personally feel you need covering in your life?

3. What happens when people remove themselves from their covering?

4. What are the main causes for a person to leave his/her covering?

Memory Verse:

Ecclesiastes 10:4

Church Government

Introduction

The Church of Jesus Christ is first of all a living spiritual organism, then, in a limited sense, an organization. If either area is neglected, the Church will be weak. To maintain the spiritual organism, there must be structure and government. Nowhere in the Word of God is an unorganized Local Church seen or taught. God is a God of order, design and structure. Some Churches have developed their structure into an administrative machine, well-oiled, but spiritually powerless. We must develop a spiritual living organism with biblical structure to have a well balanced Local Church.

I. The Need for Government

    A. Because of _____.

    B. Because of _____.

II. Three Main Channels of God's Government

    A. _____ *1 Cor 11:1-3*

    B. _____ *Rom 13*

    C. _____ *Heb 13:17; 1 Cor 12:28*

III. The Government of the Church

    A. It must be understood that the New Testament Local Church was an autonomous local assembly. By autonomous, we mean self-governing, self-supporting, and self-propagating. The autonomous Local Church is free from ecclesiastical authority outside of its own Church structure. The New Testament says nothing of a headquarters with a ruling body of district overseers who control the Local Church. Government of the Local Church must come from within that Church with a ruling body of God-ordained Elders.

B. Two New Testament office – *Phil 1:1*

1. _____

2. _____

IV. The Office and Ministry of Bishops

A. There are three main words used in the New Testament for the office and work of the bishop.

1. _____ (Greek, *presbyteros* — *"a senior; not a novice"*)

2. _____ (Greek, *episcopos* — *"to oversee, a watchman; one who rules over"*)

3. _____ (Greek, *poimen* — *"shepherd; one who feeds, protects and guards"*)

B. The Scripture teaches a plurality of ruling Elders in Local Churches. This is for the purpose of shepherding the people, and also giving checks and balances to the Senior Pastor who would be considered as the ruling Elder or the first among equals.

1. *Acts 14:23* – elders in every Church

2. *Acts 15:4-23* – elders in the Jerusalem Church

3. *Acts 16:4* – elders in the Jerusalem Church

4. *Acts 20:17* – elders in the Ephesus Church

5. *1 Tm 5:1, 17-21* – let the elders rule

6. *Jas 5:14* – call for the elders of the Church

7. *1 Pt 5:1* – the elders which are among you

8. *Heb 13:17* – obey them that have the rule over you

C. The qualifications of a bishop — *1 Tm 3:1-13*

V. The Office and Ministry of Deacons

A. Deacon:— Greek, *"to serve, to minister unto in practical or spiritual things."*
1 Tm 3:8; Phil 1:1; Mk 9:35; 10:43-45

B. The spirit of a deacon – *Mk 10:43-45*

C. The office of a deacon — *Acts 6:1-6; 1 Tm 3:8-11*

D. The qualifications of a deacon — *1 Tm 3:8-11*

    1. Relationship to character and spiritual matters

        (a) *Good reputation as a Christian — Acts 6:3*

        (b) *Spiritual - full of the Holy Spirit — Acts 6:3*

        (d) *Sound spiritual judgment, full of wisdom — Acts 6:3*

    2. Relationship to the Church

        (a) *Acceptable to the Church — Acts 6:5*

        (b) *Acceptable to the Elders — Acts 6:6*

        (c) *Set apart by prayer and laying on of hands — Acts 6:6*

    3. Relationship to Personal Life

        (a) *Serious — 1 Tm 3:8*

        (b) *Not double-tongued — 1 Tm 3:8*

        (c) *Not given to drink — 1 Tm 3:8*

        (d) *Not greedy for gain — 1 Tm 3:8*

    4. Relationship to the Ministry

        (a) *Loyal to Word and conscience — 1 Tm 3:9*

        (b) *Proven men — 1 Tm 3:10*

        (c) *Blameless — 1 Tm 3:10*

        (d) *Faithful in all things — 1 Tm 3:11*

    5. Relationship to the Family

        (a) *Responsibilities of the wife — 1 Tm 3:11*

        (b) *Husband of one wife — 1 Tm 3:12*

        (c) *Must manage children and household well — 1 Tm 3:12*

Conclusion — blessings of a deacon's ministry — 1 Tm 3:13

Questions:

1. What are the three main channels for God's government?

2. Describe in your own words what an autonomous Local Church is.

3. What is the government of a Local Church? Who is in charge?

4. What is the difference between an Elder and a Deacon?

Memory Verse:

Hebrews 13:17

Relationship of Sheep to Shepherd

Introduction

The picture of the shepherd and the sheep is a picture of warmth and beauty in which love, compassion and beauty is exchanged. The sheep need protection from would-be destroyers more than any other animal. There are numerous biblical reasons why God has chosen this animal in describing His own people. Our behavior patterns and life habits are so much like that of sheep, it is well nigh embarrassing!

I. Biblical Symbols of the Believer

A. The Believer is pictured as a _____. *1 Jn 2:1*

B. The Believer is pictured as a _____. *Gal 4:1-6*

C. The Believer is pictured as a _____. *Jn 15:1-10*

D. The Believer is pictured as a _____. *2 Tm 2:20-21*

E. The Believer is pictured as a _____. *2 Tm 2:3; Eph 6:12-17*

F. The Believer is pictured as a _____. *1 Cor 12:14-27*

G. The Believer is pictured as a _____. *1 Cor 3:16*

H. The Believer is pictured as a _____. *1 Pt 2:5-9*

I. The Believer is pictured as a _____.
Pss 78:52; 79:13; 95:7; 100:3; 119:176; Is 53:6; Mt 9:36

II. The Sheep in Relationship to the Chief Shepherd

1 Peter 2:25 "For you were like sheep going astray, but now you have returned to the shepherd and overseer of your souls"

1 Peter 5:4 "And when the chief shepherd appears, you will receive the crown of glory that will never fade away."

John 10:11 "I am the good shepherd; the good shepherd lays down his life for his sheep."

Hebrews 13:20 "Jesus, the great shepherd of the sheep"

A. _____ *"The Lord is my shepherd"*

B. _____ *"I shall lack nothing"*

C. _____ *"He makes me lie down in green pastures"*

D. _____ *"He leads me beside still waters"*

E. _____ *"Your rod and your staff they comfort me"*

F. _____ *"You anoint my head with oil"*

III The Sheep in Relationship to the Under-Shepherd

A. Scriptures denoting a *"set man"* as a shepherd

1. *Nm 27:15-17 "Set a man over the congregation ... that the congregation of the Lord be not as sheep which have no shepherd"*

2. *1 Kgs 22:17 "I saw all Israel scattered upon the hills as sheep that have no shepherd"*

3. *Zec 10:2 "They were troubled because there was no shepherd"*

4. *Zec 13:7 "Smite the shepherd and the sheep will be scattered"*

5. *Eph 4:11 "and He gave some to be shepherds"*

B. Responsibility of the sheep

1. Must recognize its helpless and defenseless state without a shepherd to watch over it.

2. Must recognize its nature to go astray or wander, with no sense to find its way back to safety.

3. Must recognize that its safety is to stay with the flock under the guidance and protection of the shepherd.

4. Must recognize its need of a sheepfold, or local Church.
   (Sheepfold:— Hebrew, *"hedged or fenced place, restrained place"*)

5. Must recognize and respond to the rod and staff of the shepherd, thus acknowledging his love, discipline and care for the welfare of the sheep.

6. Must recognize and respond to the shepherd's voice.

7. Must realize that wool is to be given; otherwise sheep will become blind and will soon die.

8. Must recognize the purpose of the sheep is to reproduce lambs into the fold.

C. Identifying problem sheep

1. The solitary sheep
2. The hermit sheep
3. The wandering sheep
4. The *"cast"* sheep
5. The Judas sheep

Questions:

1. What picture comes to your mind when we speak of shepherd and sheep?

2. What specific point do you identify with *Psalm 23?*

3. How can we as sheep better the relationship between us and our earthly shepherd?

4. Which one of the problem sheep specifically spoke to you and how?

Memory Verse:

1 Peter 2:25

Relationship of Shepherd to Sheep

Introduction

There are many people who have attended Church all their lives without really knowing what a Pastor/shepherd is. They have used the title "Pastor" when addressing certain ministries in the Church without understanding the special place this local ministry should have in their life. The Pastor/shepherd is different from the Apostle, Prophet, Evangelist or Teacher because of what he does and how he does it. We will discover in this lesson the role of the local Pastor/shepherd, his responsibilities, relationships and unique ministry he has to the sheep.

I. Titles Denoting the Servant of the Lord

A. _____ *1 Tm 3:1-2; Ti 1:7; Phil 1:1*

B. _____ *1 Tm 5:1, 17; Ti 1:5; Jas 5:14*

C. _____ *Heb 2:17; 1 Pt 2:5-9*

D. _____ *Rom 10:14; 1 Tm 2:7*

E. _____ *Eph 3:7, 6:21; Col 1:7, 23, 25; 4:7*

F. _____ *Eph 4:11-12; Mk 6:34; Mt 9:36-37*

1. Pastor:— Greek, *poimen* — *"a shepherd, a feeder"*

2. Feed:— Greek, *poimaino* — *"to tend as a shepherd"*

3. Rule:— Greek, *poimaino* — *"to shepherd, guide or govern"*

4. Shepherd: — Greek, *poimen* — *"to shepherd or feed"*
   Hebrew, *ra'ah* — *"to lead to pasture or to grazing, to rule or associate with as a companion"*

5. The Pastor is responsible for a particular flock; he establishes relationships of personal involvement with individuals; he seldom develops a reputation as the specialist but confines himself to local concerns; seeing his sheep develop toward maturity is his main reward in life.

II. The Need for True Shepherds

A. The danger of false shepherds

Jer 10-21; 23:1-10; Ez 34:1-10

1. _____ *Ez 34:1*

2. _____ *Ez 34:12*

3. _____ *Ez 34:4*

4. _____ *Ez 34:4*

5. _____ *Ez 34:5*

B. The danger of the day we are living in

1. Day of great scattering — *Ez 34:12*
2. Day of darkness and gloominess — *Ez 34:12*
3. Day of Satanic attack — *Ez 34:5-6*
4. Day of independent spirit — *Ps 68:6*

III. The Responsibilities of True Shepherds

Eph 4:11-12; Is 40:10-11

A. The shepherd is a _____ of the sheep. *Gn 4:2; 1 Sm 17:20-22*

Keeper: — Hebrew, *"to look upon, to watch with pleasure to delight in,"* watchful care and attention to the spiritual and practical needs of the sheep.

1. You cannot be a keeper of something you have not received. There must be a commitment between the shepherd and the sheep. *Jn 6:37-39*

2. A keeper is one who will watch over the sheep with pleasure. This is made possible by the attitude take by the sheep. *Heb 13:17* — obedience and submission.

B. The shepherd is the _____.
Jas 5:9; Jn 10:2-3, 7-9; Ps 84:10

The sheep were gathered into the sheepfold, and the doorway was guarded by the shepherd. The door is used to screen out and keep out that which will harm the flock.

1. The shepherd must establish doctrines or teaching that will and shape the flock of God.

2. The shepherd must set the moral and spiritual standards of the flock so as to protect the whole flock.

3. The shepherd must screen carefully those who are brought into the flock to see if there would be harmful influences coming into the sheepfold; this is done through the *"door"* of teaching. The Church Life class is used to prove the sincerity and genuineness of the sheep coming into the flock.

C. The shepherd is the _____.
Jn 21:15-17; Acts 20:28; 1 Pt 5:2

1. The food must be nutritional.

2. The diet must be well balanced.

D. The shepherd is the _____.
Is 53:7

This is not a cruel act, because unshorn sheep soon become a problem to themselves. Too much wool on a sheep will cause the animal to collect mud, briars, insects and tics.

1. The shearing of sheep pictures the reciprocal relationship which must exist between God's people and the Pastor. *Lk 6:38; Prv 11:24-25*

2. The shearing of sheep speaks of the shepherd taking from the sheep that which potentially could hurt the sheep.

II.   The Ingredients of a Healthy Shepherd-Sheep Relationship

A. When the Shepherd is fulfilling his role according to Scriptural command, supplying for sheep a balanced diet, secure protection, and joyful, peaceful atmosphere where love is expressed and received.

B. When the sheep are joyfully obeying the Biblical principles and teachings of the shepherd, responding to the shearing time with Godly expectation, and following the shepherd with Biblical support and faith.

Questions:

1. How have you perceived the *"Pastor"* in time past?

2. What is this lesson spoken to you specifically concerning the role and function of the Pastor?

3. What can you do to make your relationship to the shepherd more effective?

4. What is one specific area in you life that could hinder you from being a healthy sheep?

Memory Verse:

Isaiah 40:11

LESSON 12
Restoration #1

Introduction

The Apostle Paul in the Epistle to the Romans states that we are called according to His purpose. I would be of great spiritual benefit for God's people to understand what God's purpose is. Is God's divine purpose to *"renew,"* or to *"restore?"* What is the Spirit saying to the Church now, today? If God wanted only to renew all existing dead denominational churches, which one then is the pattern church that we are to follow? We believe God is restoring the Church to His original blueprint, His original purpose. That is why there is so much shaking going on in the religious world today. God is saying, *"Restore!"* Is 42:22; Acts 3:19-21

I. Definition of the Word "Restoration"

A. Hebrew, *"to restore something that has been stolen, taken in violence"*

B. Greek, *"to reconstruct, to set something back in order, to return to the original state, to restore it to the full power and glory of the former state, to repair, to renew"*

C. Summary: Spiritually speaking, restoration is the returning to a former position or condition by renewing or restoring that which has been taken away. When we speak of restoration, we are speaking of God restoring all truth which has been lost, restoring that which the prophets have spoken, and all that the Church in the Book of Acts had.

II. The Need for Restoration

A. _____ *Gn 3:1-22*

B. _____ *Ex 19:1-6*

C. _____ *Mt 16:18; Acts 1:8*

III. The Old Testament Law of Restoration

The concept of restoration is exemplified in the laws God gave Israel. In the following Scriptures, we will see what God set forth as principle concerning restoration. The one main discovery is that God always restored more than was stolen, and always restored the best.

A. The law of restoration in Exodus

1. Restore _____. Ex 22:1

2. Shall make _____. Ex 22:2-3

3. Restore _____. Ex 22:4, 7-9

4. Restore _____. Ex 22:5

B. The law of restoration in Leviticus

1. Restore that which was _____, _____,

_____, _____. Lv 6:1-6

2. Restoration to take place at a specific time period _____,

restoration of _____, _____. Lv 25:8-13

C. The law of restoration in Deuteronomy and Proverbs

1. Restore all _____. Dt 22:1-3

2. Restore _____. Prv 6:31

IV. The Scope of Restoration

A. Restoration of all that was lost in the first Adam

1. _____ Gn 1:26

2. _____ Gn 1:26

3. _____ Gn 1:28

4. _____ Gn 1:28

5. _____ Gn 1:28

6. _____ *Gn 2, 3*

7. _____ *Gn 2, 3*

B. Restoration of all that the prophets have spoken – *Acts 3:19-21*

    1. _____ *Is 2:1-2*

    2. _____ *Is 2:3; 30:20-21*

    3. _____ *Hg 2:7-8*

    4. _____ *Hg 2:8-9; Is 60:*

    5. _____ *Am 9:12-13; Acts 15:13-19*

    6. _____ *Am 9:12-13; Is 2:2-3*

    7. _____ *Is 1:26; Prv 11:14; 12:20; Mk 15:43*

C. Restoration is limited by what the prophets have spoken, and what can pass through the Cross.

Questions:

1. Explain in your own words what the word *"restoration"* means to you.

2. How does the law of restoration affect what God is restoring to the Church now?

3. How do we know what cannot be restored? Will the devil be restored? Will all fallen angels be restored? Will the Old Testament temple be restored?

4. How does restoration affect you personally?

Memory Verse:

Acts 3:19-21

Restoration #2

Introduction

In this lesson, the emphasis will be placed on the restoration of the Church. How much has been stripped from the Church and how much has she lost? What can we expect to be restored to the Church before the second coming of Christ?

I. The Church Before the Decline

A. The Lord Jesus promised a strong, victorious Church – *Mt 16:16-18*

B. The Apostle Paul taught the victorious Church – *Eph 5:25-32*

C. The Church in the Book of Acts:

1. _____ *1:14; 2:1; 4:32-33*

2. _____ *2:40-42; 1:17-20*

3. _____ *1:20; 2:16, 29-30; 3:22-25; 4:23-30*

4. _____ *2:22-36*

5. _____ *2:43-47*

6. _____ *3:1-10*

7. _____ *5:1-10*

8. _____ *6:1-8*

9. _____ *8:7-8*

10. _____ *13:1-4*

11. _____ *13:2-4*

12. _____ *8:6-13, 40*

13. _____ *11:27-30; 13:1-2*

14. _____ *13:1-6*

15. _____ *15:1-4*

16. _____ *20:28*

17. _____ *15:2, 5*

18. _____ *8:8; 19:1-20*

II. The Causes of the Decline

A. Lost their single eye—*Rev 3:18; Gn 3:1-7*

B. Left their first love—*Rev 2:4; 1 Jn 4:18*

C. Lukewarmness—*Rev 3:15-16*

D. Allowed false teachers to go uncorrected—*Rev 2:14-15; 2 Pt 2:1*

E. Allowed false prophets to go uncorrected—*Rev 2:20-23*

F. Complacency, worldliness and mixture—*Rev 3:17; 1 Jn 2:15-17*

III. The Decline as Seen in Church History

A. Dark Ages of the Church – AD 500-1200
   1. Rise of ritualism and formalism.
   2. Dependence on and worship of tradition.
   3. Emphasis on the cathedral buildings.

B. Loss of truths from the Church (67 AD – 1200 AD)

   67   —   Nero burns Rome; great persecution of the Christians

   100   —   Last Apostle (John) now dead; zenith of Roman prosperity

   110   —   Early Church Fathers persecuted

   130   —   Laying on of hands

   140   —   Prophets

   150   —   Gifts of the Spirit lost, Latin becomes language of western Church

   160   —   Plurality of eldership

180 — NT canon of Scripture nearly completed

185 — Christianity most dominant religion

187 — Local Church autonomy threatened

188 — First infant baptism by sprinkling

200 — Priesthood of higher order; ministers called "priest"

240 — Double standard of holiness; rise of monasticism

250 — Clergy elected by outside authority

284 — Diocletian persecutes Christians, thought himself to be a sun-god

300 — Justification by faith replaced by works

313 — Rise of the Imperial Church; Constantine ends Christian persecution: edict of Milan; toleration of free worship

325 — Easter Sunday decreed by Council of Nicea

327 — State control of Church

340 — Church mixture: Greek and oriental philosophies mixed with Christianity: ceremonies had outward splendor that belonged to heathen temples

341 — Rome splits, east and west, two Empires

350 — Christmas Day festivals established

352 — Much doctrinal confusion; error, heresy on the rise

360 — Scrolls replaced by books; Church drawing up canon of Scripture, agreed on 22 books

380 — Edict of Theodosius; abolished crucifixion, gladiator fighting, killing of unwanted children; destroyed heathen temples

397 — New Testament books canonized at the Council of Carthage

400 — Separation of Clergy and laity

405 — Latin Vulgate translated for Catholic Church

438 — Unlawful to disagree with beliefs of Catholic Church of Rome

440 — Celibacy became a law of the Roman Catholic Church for the priests

450 — "Mary" placed as head of all saints; many festivals and worship

476 — Fall of the Western Roman Empire

496 — Prayers, chants and mass instructions

517 — Emperor Wunti becomes a Buddhist, introduces new religion to China

570 — Mohammed, founder of Islam, claimed o be last of the prophets

500-1200 Church has become paganized with worship of images, relics, martyrs, saints, Mary, angels, separation of clergy and laity with monasticism and great confusion doctrinally, putting the Church into the age commonly called the *"Dark Ages."*

IV. The Restoration of the Church (Reformation) – Is 28:9-13

A. Restoration of _____ :— Martin Luther, 1438-1546 AD

B. Restoration of _____ in common language:— William Tyndale, 1536 AD;— King James Version, 1607 AD

C. Restoration of _____ by immersion:— Anabaptists, 1525-40 AD: The leaders were Hubmier, Grabel, Mantz—*"the dunkers"*.

D. Restoration of _____ :— Zinzendorf, Spencer, John Wesley, George Whitefield; 1630-1738 AD.

E. Restoration of _____ :— A.B. Simpson; 1840 AD

F. Restoration of _____ :— Jeffrey brothers in England, Azusa Street revival in Los Angeles, Welsh revival; 1900-1906 AD

G. Restoration of _____ and _____ :— Canadian revival; 1949 AD

V. Decline and Restoration Illustrated

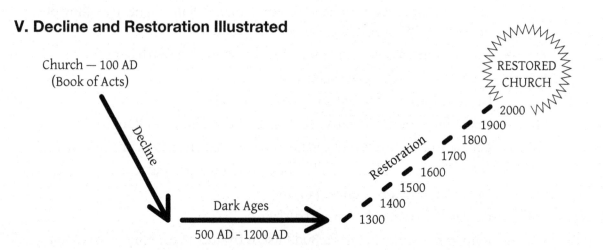

Summary

- Restoration is recovery of divine principles believed, taught and experienced by the Early Church. *Eph 2:20; 1 Cor 3:10; 1 Tm 4:6*

- Restoration is the renewal of spiritual life in the church because of restored truths. *1 Tm 4:15-16*

- Restoration is bringing into existence all things predicted by the prophets. *Acts 3:21; Rom 16:26*

Questions:

1. What kind of Church does the New Testament promise will be in existence when Jesus comes again?

2. Sum up the Church of the first century in three words.

3. Explain in your own words the cause for the Church to decline into the Dark Ages.

4. What will the restored Church be like?

Memory Verse:

Ephesians 5:27

LESSON 14
Gifts and Ministries

Introduction

The Body of Christ is to manifest Christ to the world, and is also to serve the Head of the Body, the Lord Jesus Christ. All powers proceed from the Holy Spirit — no member may boast against another; no member, however insignificant, may consider himself unessential, but is equally obligated to be yielded to the Holy Spirit.

I. The Many-Membered Body of Christ

A. First the natural, then the spiritual — *1 Cor 15:45-47*

   1. The natural body has _____ .

   2. The natural body has _____ , each one with a different unique function.

   3. The natural body has _____ because of each member's willingness to work together.

   4. The natural body _____ and _____ the need for other functioning parts of the body.

B. The spiritual Body of Christ

   1. The spiritual Body has one head, the Lord Jesus Christ — *1 Cor 11:1-3*

   2. The spiritual Body has many members, each with a different responsibility to the whole body — *1 Cor 12:12, 14, 20*

   3. The spiritual Body is governed by the Holy Spirit, and it is he who places each member into the body — *1 Cor 12:18, 15-17, 21-24*

   4. The spiritual Body functions because of the care each member has one for another — *1 Cor 12:24-26*

II. The Spiritual Gifts Given to the Body

1 Cor 12:1-8 "for to one is given by the Spirit..."

1 Cor 12:2 "concerning spiritual gifts, I would not have you ignorant"

A. Gift:— Greek, *charis, charisma* —"*a gift given out of good will, a gift involving grace on the part of God as the donor*"; the root word "*char*" indicates things which produce well being, beneficial, highly valuable. The word "*charis*" is used 155 times in the New Testament, mostly a Pauline expression.

B. The nine Gifts of the Spirit

1. _____ *1 Cor 12:8; Prv 8:22-30; 2 Pt 3:15*

   "*An unearned supernatural impartation of fragment of God's total wisdom to meet a particular need, or answer a particular challenge*"

2. _____ *1 Cor 12:8; Hos 12:10; Acts 13:9-11*

   "*God given ability to receive from God by revelation the knowledge of facts and information which is humanly impossible to know*"

3. _____ *1 Cor 12:9; Acts 3:4-16; Rom 15:18-19*

   "*This is not just believing faith as received at salvation, but this faith is a special faith, imparted by God for the impossible situation.*"

4. _____ *1 Cor 12:9; Acts 14:8-11; 5:15; 28:8-10*

   Note the word "*gifts*" here is plural – healing for the body, soul and spirit, healing for the total man. This is a God-given ability to minister healing to any part of man.

5. _____ *1 Cor 12:10; Acts 20:4-12*

   "*The imparted power of the Holy Spirit to do that which could not be produced by natural agents and means, defies reason and transcends natural laws*"

6. _____ *1 Cor 12:10; 14:6; Rev 19:10*

   In Scripture there are three levels of prophecy: spirit, gift and office of the prophet.

   Here we have the gift, which is for edification, exhortation and comfort.

7. _____ *1 Cor 12:10; Acts 16:16-18*

   This gift is used to discern the activities and manifestations of spirits, whether good or evil, and the ability to deal with them.

8. _____ *1 Cor 12:10; 14:18; Acts 2:1-17*

   • *Initial evidence of having received Baptism of Holy Spirit*

   • *Devotional tongues which is praying and praising God in tongues in your prayer closet, or the prayer room — 1 Cor 14:2, 4*

   • *Here we have the gift of tongues used for the edifying of the corporate Body of Christ in the Local Church — 1 Cor 12:10, 28-30; 14:5, 13, 22, 26-27*

9. _____ *1 Cor 12:10; 14:13*

   This is the God given ability to bring forth in a known tongue a message that was given in an unknown tongue.

C. Prerequisites to moving in the Gifts of the Holy Spirit

The most commonly used chapters used to teach on the Gifts of the Spirit are *1 Corinthians 12* and *14*. When the Apostle Paul brought this teaching to the Corinthian Church, he laid a solid foundation in the first eleven chapters before dealing with the Gifts of the Spirit. I suggest that we should examine the eleven chapters and teach the principles found therein prior to teaching the chapters dealing with Gifts of the Spirit. Once the attitudes that are found in the first eleven chapters are taught and recognized, moving in Body ministry will be sound and healthy.

1. Must be properly *born again* — *Jn 3:1-12*
2. *Must be living* and *drinking* in the Holy Spirit — *Jn 7:37-39*
3. Must be in *proper relationship* to the Body — *1 Cor 8:*
4. Must be in proper relationship to the *Head of the Body,* the Lord Jesus Christ.
5. Must be willing to receive *correction* and *adjustment* from Godly placed leadership.
6. Must be *set apart* and *consecrated* in your life-style and habits.
7. Must understand that *love edifies.*
8. Must have *pure motivation* for ministering the Gifts.
9. Must *covet earnestly* the best gifts, and must desire to be used of God in this way. *1 Pt 4:10; 1 Cor 8:1-3; 12:31.*

Questions:

1. What does the natural body teach us about the spiritual body?

2. What places the members into their particular place?

3. Which Gift of the Spirit do you desire and covet after? Which gift have you received and presently use?

4. Discuss the prerequisites to moving in the Gifts of the Spirit. How do these apply to our own local assembly?

Memory Verse:

1 Corinthians 12:31

LESSON 15
The Five-Fold Ministries

Introduction

Read *Ephesians 4:1-16*. In this lesson, we will concentrate our efforts on the *Epistle to the Ephesian Church*. This *Epistle* can be divided into to sections: *chapters 1-3* dealing mainly with *doctrine* and the *Church* worldwide, and *chapters 4-6* dealing mainly with *practical* subjects and the Believer's responsibility in *service* and *walk* in four areas: the Church, the world, the home, and spiritual warfare. The one segment we will examine will be the five ascension gift ministries given to the Church, their purpose, specific function and a working definition of each.

I. The Believer's Walk and Service

A. Exhortation to walk in our calling — *Eph 4:1*

1. Walk _____ *Eph 4:1*

2. Walk _____ *Eph 4:2*

3. Walk _____ *Eph 4:2*

4. Walk _____ *Eph 4:2*

5. Walk _____ *Eph 4:2*

6. Walk _____ *Eph 4:2*

7. Walk _____ *Eph 4:3*

8. Walk _____ *Eph 4:3-6*

9. Walk _____ *Eph 4:3*

10. Walk _____ *Eph 4:17*

11. Walk _____ *Eph 5:8*

12. Walk _____ *Eph 5:15*

B. Receiving the Grace of God — *Eph 4:7*

1. All members have received a measure of grace — *Rom 12:5-7*

2. All members must recognize their God-given grace.

II. The Five Ascension Gift Ministries

A. He gave gifts unto men — *Eph 4:8-10*

1. Ministries are given, not self-appointed. Men do not choose their gift or calling, but God must impart gifts unto men.

    - *Acts 13:14 "The Holy Spirit said, separate unto me Barnabas and Paul for the work whereunto I have called them . . ."*

    - *Eph 3:1 "Wherefore I was made a minister according to the gift of the grace of God given unto me . . ."*

    - *1 Tim 1:12 "And I thank Christ Jesus our Lord who hath enabled me, for that he counted me faithful, putting me into the ministry"*

2. Ministries are not imparted to angels or gods, or men of a special sinless nature, but God imparts gifts unto flesh and blood, real men, with their faults, carnalities and shortcomings. *Rom 7:1-20*

B. Defining the five ascension gift ministries — *Eph 4:11*

1. _____

    Greek, *apostolos* — *"one sent forth as a messenger or ambassador"*

    (a) *Christ was an Apostle — Heb 3:1; Jn 20:21*

    (b) *The twelve Apostles of Christ — Mt 10:2*

    (c) *The Apostles mentioned in the New Testament — Andronicus, Rom 16:7; Junia, Rom 16:7; James, Gal 1:19; Barnabas, Acts 4:36; Paul, Acts 14:14; Titus, 2 Cor 8:23; Epaphroditus, Phil 2:25; Timothy, 1 Thes 1:1; Silvanus, 1 Thes 2:6; Apollas, 1 Cor 4:6, 9*

    (d) *The ministry of an Apostle is used to establish new Churches, is a sign gift ministry, has authority as a spiritual father to bring correction to Local Churches, and he is able to function as a Pastor, Teacher, Prophet, or Evangelist.*

2. _____

Greek, *prophetes* — *"one who speaks for another; one who speaks for God"*

   (a) *Christ was a Prophet — Lk 24:19; Deut 18:18; John 3:34*

   (b) *Prophets mentioned in the New Testament — Acts 11:27-30, 21:8-11, 15:32, 15:41, 13:1-3 — Agabus, Simeon, Lucius, Manaen, Saul, Judas, Silas*

   (c) *The ministry of a Prophet is also to help establish new Churches; a seer or one who is able to receive information from God so as to give counsel, direction and rebuke to the Body of Christ.*

3. _____

Greek, *euangelistes* — *"messenger of good news; to bring glad tidings by preaching"*

   (a) *Christ was an Evangelist — Lk 4:18-19; Mt 4:23*

   (b) *Evangelists in the New Testament — Philip; Acts 21:8, 8:1-35*

   (c) *The ministry of the Evangelist is more than ministering salvation to the unsaved. The Evangelist is given to the Church in Ephesians 4:11. We also see a tremendous example of an Evangelist in Philip — he preached Christ, he had the ministry of healing and miracles, and he knew the word of God.*

4. _____

Greek, *poimen* — *"shepherd, or one who feeds the flock; protects and provides"*

   (a) *Christ was a Pator — Jn 10:11; Heb 13:20; 1 Pt 5:4*

   (b) *Pastors in the New Testament — Eph 4:11; 1 Tm; 2 Tm; Ti. Timothy, Pastor of the large Ephesus Church; Titus, Pastor in Crete; James, Pastor at Jerusalem.*

   (c) *The ministry of the Pastor is to feed, protect, discern needs of the sheep in a given locality.*

   Note: "bishop" refers to the office; "elder" refers to the man; "pastor" refres to his work. All Elders, those who rule, do not hold the office of pastor, but all Elders must have a shepherd's heart and be apt to feed. All Pastors must be qualified Elders.

5. _____

Greek, *didaskalos* — *"to hold discourse with others in order to instruct them; the addition which the teacher makes to the knowledge of the one he teaches; to train, educate, disciple."*

(a) *Christ was a Teacher — Jn 3:2*

(b) *Teachers in the New Testament — Acts 15:1-2; 13:1-15; 1 Cor 12:28; Rom 12:6-8*

The ministry of the Teacher is to unfold and clearly expound the Word of God to others. The teacher must be able to bring balance by his teaching into the Local Assembly. All Elders must be able to teach in order to establish the people of God. Acts 20:28; Eph 4:14; 1 Tm 5:17; Ti 1:9; 2 Tm 2:2

III. The Purpose of the Five Ascension Gift Ministries

A. Five ascension Gift Ministries are for the purpose of _____.

Apostle
Prophet
Pastor — for | equipping of the saints | unto the ⟨ work of the ministry
Evangelist   edifying of the Body
Teacher

B. Five ascension gift ministries are for the purpose of _____

_____.

Eph 4:13

C. Five ascension gift ministries are for the purpose of bringing the Body to

_____.

Eph 4:13

D. Five ascension gift ministries are for the purpose of bringing _____

_____.

Eph 4:14

E. Five ascension gift ministries are for the purpose of _____

_____.

Eph 4:15-16

F. Five ascension gift ministries are for the purpose of _____

_____.

Questions:

1. What have all members of the Body of Christ received?

2. How does one receive a calling to the five-fold ministry?

3. Summarize in one statement each one of the five-fold ministries.

4. What is the purpose of the five-fold ministry?

Memory Verse:

Ephesians 4:11-12

Stewardship

Introduction

This lesson will develop the teaching and concept of Christian stewardship. Stewardship speaks of the Christian's responsibility to administrate and manage all things Christ has delegated into our hands.

I. Definition and Cultural Background of Stewardship

A. Greek, *"The management of a household or of household affairs. Specifically the management, oversight or administrator of another's property; to act as the superintendent."*

   1. *epitropos* — *"one to whose care or honor one has been entrusted, acurator or guardian."* Mt 20:8; Gal 4:2

   2. *oikonomos* — *"a manager, a superintendent; made up of two Greek words, oikos (have) and meno (to dispense or to manage)."* *This word is used to describe the function of delegated responsibility, as in the parables of the laborers and the unjust steward.*

   3. translated as — dispensation — *1 Cor 9:17; Eph 1:10; 3:2; Col 1:25*

      edifying — *1 Tm 1:4*

      chamberlain — *Rom 16:23*

      governors — *Gal 4:2*

B. English, *"A man entrusted with the management of the household or estate of another; one employed to manage the domestic affairs, superintend the servants, collect the rents or incomes, keep the accounts. One who acts as supervisor or administrator of the finances and property for another."* (Webster's Dictionary)

C. Background — During the time of the writings of the New Testament books, the word *"oikonomos"* or steward was freely used in everyday vernacular. This word described the function of a certain class of trusted slaves who were highly coveted by wealthy estate owners. These slaves, who were usually captured during the many battles the Romans had, were usually very intelligent, gifted men who could work as an administrator of the estate.

II. Stewardship in the Old Testament

A. _____ the steward of Abraham. *Gn 15:2; 24:1-67*

B. _____ the steward for Laban. *Gn 29; 30:25-43*

C. _____ the steward for Potiphar. *Gn 39:4-5; 44:1-4*

D. _____ The steward of King Elah. *1 Kgs 16:8-9*

III. Stewardship in the New Testament

A. Parable of _____. *Lk 16:1-13*

B. Parable of _____. *Lk 19:12-27; Mt 25:14-30*

C. Parable of _____. *Mt 21:33-46*

D. Parable of _____. *Lk 12:35-48*

Note: *Each parable teaches the same principle of individual responsibility for what one has received. What we do with our time, money, talents, ministry, and possessions is of great importance to the Lord of the house. (Heb 3:1-6)* We are not owners of all that God has given us; we are stewards and managers and therefore accountable as to how we handle His wealth and His blessings.

IV. Stewardship of the Believer

1 Cor 4:1-2; 1 Pt 4:10; Mt 6:19-21

A. _____ *Col 3:1-2; 1 Tm 6:7-10*

1. The Gospels contain more warnings against money and its misuses than any other subject.

2. The first Apostle to fall was connected with the problem of money; he sold Christ for money that he never lived to spend. *Mt 25:4-16*

3. The first sin in the Early Church was connected with money and the giving of it unto the Lord. *Acts 5:1-10*

B. _____ *Mal 3:8; Prv 3:9-10; Lk 6:38*

1. Definition of tithing (Hebrew, *maser*) (Greek, *deka*)

The word *"Tithe"* translates in Hebrew and Greek words that mean a tenth, or to give a tenth of something. In the Old Testament the tenth was usually considered that part of the produce, flock or herds due from a worshipper to his God for the support of the Sanctuary and the priest.

2. Tithing in the Old Testament.

(a) *Abraham pays tithes to Melchizedek — Gn 14:18-20*

(b) *Jacob makes a covenant with God to pay tithes — Gn 28:22*

(c) *Nation of Israel practiced tithing — Lv 27:30-33; Nm 18:20-24; Neh 10:37; Dt 12:11*

3. Tithing in the New Testament

(a) *Jesus confirmed tithing — Mt 23:23; Lk 11:42; 18:12; Heb 7:1-21; Mt 5:20*

(b) *Paul taught tithing — 1 Cor 16:1-2*

C. _____ *Mal 3:8*

Offerings are different from tithing. Offerings are the free will acts of the individual to give whatever amount the Lord lays on your heart. But the Bible says we are to give offerings. We can rob God if we do not obey this command. *Phil 4:15-18*

D. Excuses and reasons why some Christians do not tithe

1. Tithing is an Old Testament doctrine, therefore I should live under grace and not law. (The problem with this is that Jesus said "give everything." Tithing is the minimum!)

2. I need all the money I make to live on; I cannot afford to pay 10% of my income. (I am basically selfish.)

3. I would like to pay tithes, and some day I know I will pay tithes, but right now I have bought so many things on credit and time payments that I have no other choice but to continue to *rob* God.

4. I would love to tithe *but* I just don't know if I have enough faith to live on 90% of my income.

Questions:

1. What does stewardship mean to you?

2. What has God put into your hands that you are responsible for?

3. What does the Bible teach concerning tithing?

4. What part of this lesson has convicted or challenged your life?

Memory Verse:

Malachi 3:8

LESSON 17
Prayer and Fasting

Introduction

One of the most effective ways to increase your spiritual alertness is to combine prayer and fasting. Fasting and prayer is the most powerful weapon the Lord has given to the Christian.

I. Background and Definition of Fasting

A. Hebrew, *"to afflict the soul, to bring self into discipline, affliction, to humble the soul, to mortify oneself"*

B. Greek, *"to be emptied, one who willingly abstains from food"*

C. English, *"to abstain from food for a chosen duration of time"*

D. Greek cultural — the original and most powerful motive for fasting in the Greek world is to be found in the fear of demons, spiritual powers or forces that gained power over people by eating. Fasting was one way to bring spiritual powers down and under control. Fasting was also used to prepare the worshipper to approach his deity for the reception of spiritual powers. The Greeks had a strong conviction that fasting could war off evil spirits.

E. Conceptual definition — the voluntary refraining from food and drink at a time and for a time to give oneself the opportunity to give full attention to a particular spiritual matter. To deliberately abstain from food for spiritual purposes.

II. Three Levels of Fasting

A. The _____ fast — to drink water only

B. The _____ fast — to eat certain meals only

C. The _____ fast — to eat nothing and drink nothing

III. The Sermon on the Mount

Mt 5-6-7

A. The _____
    Mt 6:1-4, "when you give your alms ... not as hypocrites" — REWARD

B. The _____
    Mt 6:5-15, "when you pray ... not as hypocrites" — REWARD

C. The life of _____
    Mt 6:16-18, "when you fast ... not as hypocrites" — REWARD

In each of these teachings, Jesus never says "IF." He says "WHEN." Jesus expected all of His followers to give to the poor, have a life of prayer, and also a life of fasting. He does not make fasting optional.

IV. The Biblical Examples of Fasting

A. Old Testament examples

    1. Moses fasted twice for 40 days without food or water.

    2. The nation of Israel fasted at least one day a year together, the Day of Atonement *(Lev 16)*.

    3. Esther fasted to save a nation from destruction. *(Est 4:1-3, 15-17)*

    4. David fasted continually to find direction and help. *(Ps 35:13)*

    5. Jehoshaphat fasted in a national crisis. *(2 Chr 20:1-30)*

    6. Ezra fasted for divine protection and guidance. *(Ez 8:21, 23)*

    7. Nehemiah fasted for divine wisdom for restoration of the walls and gates. *(Neh 1-2)*

B. New Testament examples

    1. Anna, the prophetess *(Lk 2:35-39)*

    2. Jesus *(Mt 4:1-2)*

    3. The Early Church *(Acts 13:1-4; 14:21)*

    4. The Apostle Paul *(2 Cor 6:5; 11:27)*

V. The Purpose of Fasting

Zec 7:5; Acts 13:2

A. To prepare oneself to receive from God a special word of direction.

B. To humble the soul, the soul being the rebellious part of man. You are saying to yourself—soul, you cannot have your own way any longer, you are not the master, you are the servant.

C. To afflict your soul.

D. To empty yourself and make room for the Holy Spirit to have His way.

E. To purify your spirit and life before God.

F. To loose the bonds of wickedness, undo the heavy bands of the yoke of sin and to let the oppressed go free.

VI. Prayer

1 Sm 12:33; Is 56:7; Lk 18:1

A. Prayer is an _____. *Ps 141:1-2; Lk 1:9-11; Rev 8:3-4; 11:1*

B. Prayers can be _____. *1 Pt 3:7*

   1. when there is sin and iniquity in our life — *Is 59:1-2; Ps 66:18*

   2. when there are marital problems — *1 Pt 3:7*

   3. when there is willful and presumptuous disobedience to God's word — *Prv 28:9*

   4. when there is unforgiveness in our life — *Mt 5:23-24; 6:9-13; Mk 11:25*

   5. when we pray with selfish motivation — *Jas 4:3*

   6. when there are idols in my heart — *Ez 14:3*

   7. when there is stinginess — *Pr 21:13, Lk 6:38; 1 Jn 3:22; Phil 4:19*

   8. when there is unbelief — *Jas 1:5-7*

C. Different kinds of prayers — *Lk 11:1; Acts 2:42; Eph 6:18; Jer 33:3*

   1. _____ — *1 Sm 1:17-27; Est 5:6-7; Dn 6:7-13*

   2. _____ — *Pss 6:9; 30:8; Dn 6:11; 9:20; Acts 1:14*

   3. _____ — *Rom 8:26-34; 1 Tm 2:1; Heb 7:25*

4. _____ — *1 Cor 14:14-15; Jude 20; Rom 8:26; Eph 6:18*

5. _____ — *Ps 72; 2 Chr 20:20-22; Is 56:7-8*

D. Approaching the Throne of Grace — *Heb 4:16; Mt 25:40; Acts 3:1*

Some practical guidelines on spending one hour in prayer daily, in a step-by-step procedure, spending a possible five minutes on each step:

1. Worship, adoration and singing — *Ps 100:1; Mt 6:9*
2. Confession and cleansing of yourself before God — *Dn 9:4; Neh 1:5-11*
3. Recognition of His Lordship and character — *Ps 100:3; Neh 9:4-6*
4. Asking for daily bread — *Mt 6:11, 7:7-12*
5. Bringing your petitions, supplications, others' needs before the Lord — *Phil 4:6-7*
6. Giving thanks for answers — *Ps 100:4; Eph 1:7; 1 Thes 5:18*
7. Intercession, burden bearing — *Rom 8:26*
8. A time of meditation and listening to the Lord — *Jos 1:8*
9. Reading a portion of Scripture — *Ps 119*
10. Singing praises triumphant; proclamation of prayers being answered — *Ps 22:3-8*

Questions:

1. Summarize in your own words the Biblical meaning and purpose of fasting.
2. What exactly does fasting and prayer accomplish according to Biblical examples and Scripture?
3. Name one or two major obstacles that keep you from a consistent daily prayer life?
4. What is the most rewarding aspect of prayer and fasting to you personally?

Memory Verse:

1 John 5:15

Praise and Worship

Introduction

"But Thou art holy, O Thou that inhabitest the praises of Israel." (Ps 22:3) This is the most vital part of our worship and praise, understanding that the Lord wants to inhabit, visit and commune with us during our worship times. In this teaching, we want to lay a basic foundation for the purpose, principle and result of Bible worship.

I. Definition of Praise and Worship

A. _____ Hebrew, *yadah* — *"to use the hands, to hold up or out, to worship with extended hands"*

Hebrew, *halal* — *"to be clear, have a clear sound, to celebrate"*

B. _____ Hebrew, *schachah* — *"to depress, to prostrate in homage to the royalty of God, to bow down, fall down"*

C. _____ Hebrew, *"barak"* — to kneel, bless God as an act of adoration

D. _____ Hebrew, *samah* — *"to brighten up, be blithe, gleesome, cheerful, merry, happy"*

Hebrew, *qual* — *"to spin around under the influence of violent emotions"*

Hebrew, *alats* — *"to jump for joy, to exalt"*

Hebrew, *ranan* — *"to shout for joy or cry out, sing with a loud voice"*

II. Nine Biblical Ways to Worship

Ps 111:1 "I will praise the Lord with my whole heart"

Jn 4:25 "God is spirit, and they that worship Him must worship Him in spirit and truth"

A. _____ Ps 95:1

B. _____ Pss 51:15; 145:21

C. _____ Ps 5:11; Is 12:6

D. _____ Pss 47:1; 98:8

E. _____ Pss 134:2; 141:2

F. _____ Ps 150:3-6

G. _____ Ps 134:1

H. _____ Ps 95:6

I. _____ Ps 149:3

III. The Results and Benefits of Worship

A. Worship brings forth _____ of the Lord.
    Zec 10:1; Ps 65:9; Dt 11:10-11; Job 36:27-29

B. Worship brings forth _____ of the Holy Spirit.
    Ez 47:1-8; Jl 3:18; Ps 105:41; Jn 7:37-39; Ps 46:4

C. Worship brings forth _____ of the Lord.
    Ps 22:3; Ex 29:41-46; 2 Chr 5:13-14; Zep 3:17

D. Worship brings forth _____.
    2 Kgs 3:11-27

E. Worship brings forth _____.
    2 Chr 29:27; Col 3:16; Eph 5:19

The word "selah" used continually in the Psalms indicates a change of mood, tone or a pause, an unfolding. Do not be impatient during the worship service, but let the divine "selah" of the Holy Spirit unfold. Take time to hear from God.

F. Worship brings forth _____
    2 Chr 20:21-22; Acts 16:19-34

G. Worship brings forth _____
    Is 61:3; 42:3; Pss 25:1; 86:4

IV. Priesthood Responsibility

A. We all have the calling and responsibility to function as a New Testament priest continually. *1 Pt 2:5-9; 2 Sam 24:24*

B. We all together must bring the sacrifices of a New Testament priesthood. *1 Pt 2:5-7*

1. Sacrifice of praise — *Jer 17:26; 33:11; Heb 13:15; Acts 16:25*
2. Sacrifice of thanksgiving — *Ps 107:22; 116:17; Lv 7:12; Jon 2:9*
3. Sacrifice of joy — *Ps 27:6; Lk 6:22-23*

Questions:

1. What do the definitions of praise and worship cause us to believe concerning the emotions of worship?
2. What does it mean to worship God with all of our heart?
3. What are the greatest hindrances to true worship?
4. In what way can we improve our worship before the Lord?

Memory Verse:

John 4:24

Music and Song of the Lord

Introduction

This lesson will examine the biblical perspective of music and song of the Lord in the local church. This is an area that needs much exposure and teaching because of so much misunderstanding and misconception concerning music and singing. Church choirs and singing groups in many cases have become more of an entertainment and talent performance rather than an anointed spiritual ministry unto the Lord. We need to understand what the Scripture teaches concerning this vital ministry.

I. The Power and Importance of Music

A. Definition of "music"

English, *"The art and science of combining vocal or instrumental sounds or tones in varying melody, harmony, rhythm and timbre, especially so as to form structurally complete and emotionally expressive compositions; any rhythmic sequence of pleasing sounds."* (Webster's Dictionary)

B. Benefits of music found through human discovery

1. Music motivates people to buy through different styles.
2. Music causes greater productivity on the job.
3. Hospitals use music to create a healing and peaceful atmosphere.
4. Music is used in therapy for mental and nervous disorders.
5. Music is used to help people recall forgotten associations.
6. Music is used to govern the moods of people.
7. Music is used to free people from tension.
8. Music was used in Ancient Egypt as the principal agent in healing arts.

C. Basic principles of music evaluation

(excerpts from *Basic Youth Conflicts* seminar)

1 Thes 5:23	Basic Parts of Music	Basic drives in Music	Tension/Relaxation	Basic Effects of Imbalance
SPIRIT	MELODY *to dominate*	Spiritual drive	Rise	Tension, unfulfillment, frustration, passion, despair, depression
SOUL	HARMONY *to support the melody*	Psychological drive	Dissonance/ Consonance	Confusion, rebellion, pride, sentimentalism
BODY	RHYTHM *to be concealed in the harmony & subordinate to melody*	Physical drive	Repetition/ Variation	Sensuality, distraction

II. The Ministry of Music and Musicians

Note: Of all the ministries in the Local Church, the music ministry can be one where self can be glorified, and Christ put second. The basic principle of music ministry in the Church is that the musician must decrease and Christ must increase. The people who are called to a music ministry must have their lives in order and be blameless and living with high Christian standards. The music ministry is powerful and has a deep effect upon lives. Those ministering in this area must be an example to others in their attitudes, morals, dress and spiritual fervency.

A. The restoration of the Tabernacle of David — *Am 9:11-13; Acts 15:1-25*

1. Restoration of the _____ of God.

2. Restoration of the _____.

3. Restoration of the _____.

4. Restoration of the _____.

B. Musicians — *2 Kgs 3:14; 1 Sm 16:23; 1 Chr 25:2-3; Rev 15:1-3*

1. Musicians were _____. *1 Chr 16:4; 2 Chr 20:21*

2. Musicians _____. *1 Chr 6:31-32*

3. Musicians were _____. *1 Chr 25:1*

4. The musician's heart condition is of utmost importance:

_____ of heart — *Pss 4:7; 16:9, 13:5*

_____ of heart — *Ps 78:72*

_____ heart — *Ps 15:2*

_____ heart — *Pss 51:10; 73:1*

_____ heart — *Pss 51:17; 34:18*

5. Musicians can judge their ministry by the results, or the fruit. *Mt 7:17; Gal 5:19-23*

III. The Song of the Lord

Song of Solomon 2:9 (Berkeley version) *"The season of singing has come, the voice of the turtledove is heard in our land."* The singing of the turtledove in Palestine was the first sign of Spring and indicated that the dreary barrenness of the Winter season was over!

A. Explanation of terms
   Eph 5:18-19

Aspect of	Definitive distinction	Function of song
PSALMS	Songs of praise from Scripture or songs in the character, spirit or manner of OT Psalms.	Directed primarily to God.
HYMNS	Songs of praise of human composition on Christian themes.	Directed primarily to man as testimonial or laudatory of God.
SPIRITUAL SONGS	Songs of praise of a spontaneous or un-premeditated nature with unrehearsed melodies, sung under the impetus of the Holy Spirit.	Directed to both God and man: 1. Song of Praise --- to God 2. Song of the Lord --- to man

Diagram from *"The Song of the Lord"* by David Blomgren

B. Spiritual songs

1. Greek, *pneumatikos* — *"speaking in or by the Holy Spirit."* This Greek word is usually associated with the vocal gifts of the Spirit. *1 Cor 12:1-3; 14:37.*

2. Practical definition — Spiritual songs, or the Song of the Lord, are songs sung thruogh a human vessel who is singing by the Holy Spirit. It is a song sung under the direct unction and anointing of the Holy Spirit, and as with the vocal spiritual gifts, it is usually spontaneous, and not of human composition.

C. The nature and function of the Song of the Lord

1. The Song of the Lord is _____. *1 Cor 14:3; 1 Chr 25:1; 2 Chr 20:14, 20, 21*

   - *edification*
   - *exhortation*
   - *comfort*

2. The Song of the Lord is _____. *Col 3:16*

   - *teaching*
   - *admonishing*

3. The Song of the Lord is _____. *Col 3:16-17*

Questions:

1. In what ways has music in the Church become powerless and ritualistic?
2. What is the difference between entertainment and ministry?
3. Why is the heart of the musician so important, and how does this affect their ministry?
4. In what ways has the Song of the Lord ministered unto you?

Memory Verse:

Colossians 3:16

Communion

Introduction

We as Christians enjoy the great privilege of communing with Christ daily through the ministry of the Holy Spirit — this is very *personal*. But there is also a sacred act which each Christian can do with the *corporate* Body of Christ, taught in the Scripture as communion, or the Lord's Table. This lesson will establish the Biblical doctrine of the communion table in the Local Church body.

I. Defining the term "Communion"

A. English, *"fellowship, intercourse between two or more persons, interchange of thoughts or interests, a state of giving and receiving, agreement, concord."*

B. Greek, *koinonia* — *"fellowship, association, community, joint participation."* Translated *"fellowship"* in *Acts 2:42* and *"communion"* in *1 Cor 10:16*.

II. The Biblical scope of Communion

A. The Old Testament act of communion

　　1. The _____ — *Ex 12:1-12; Mk 14:12*

　　2. The _____ — *Lv 23*

　　3. The _____ — *Lv 2:1-16; Ex 29:41, 30:9*

　　4. The _____ — *Nm 28:7; Ex 25:23-30*

B. The New Testament act of communion

　　1. Practiced by _____ and _____ — *Mt 26:26-29*

　　2. Practiced by the _____ — *Acts 2:42*

　　3. Practiced by many other _____ — *1 Cor 11:21-34*

III. The Communion Service

A. The significance of its symbols

    1. The _____. *Ps 23:5; Rev 3:20*   _____

    2. The _____. *1 Cor 10:16,17; Mt 26:25*   _____

    3. The _____. *Mt 26:27; 1 Cor 11:25*   _____

B. The Participant's Preparation

    1. Must be a true _____, living in a New Covenant relationship with the Lord. *2 Cor 5:17*

    2. Must _____ oneself. *1 Cor 11:28* (AMP) *"Let a man thoroughly examine himself, and only when he has done so should he eat of the bread and drink of the cup." 2 Cor 13:5; Pss 26:2; 139:1-2*

    3. Must _____ ourselves. *1 Cor 11:31-32* (AMP) *"For if we searchingly examined ourselves detecting our shortcomings and recognizing our own condition, we should not be judged and penalty decreed by the divine judgment." Rom 2:16; 1 Cor 4:3*

    4. Must _____ ourselves from all unrighteousness. *2 Cor 7:1-2; 1 Jn 5:7-9; Ps 51:1-15*

    5. Must come to the Table with _____ and _____. *Heb 11:6; Rom 14:23*

C. The consequences of partaking without preparation

    1. Warning to those who would come to the Table _____. *1 Cor 11:27-29*

    2. The unprepared or unworthy will be found _____. *1 Cor 11:27*

    3. The unprepared will eat and drink _____ to himself. *1 Cor 11:29*

    4. The unprepared will receive _____ and _____ at the Table. *1 Cor 11:30*

    5. The unprepared will receive _____ from the Lord. *1 Cor 11:31-32*

IV. The Sacrament of Communion is:

    A. a divine command

    B. a blessed privilege

    C. a necessary memorial

    D. a willing testimony

    E. a humbling confession

    F. an act of faith

    G. a solemn warning

    H. a promise of divine health and healing

Questions:

1. How does the Passover in *Exodus 12* speak of a communion service? Discuss.

2. What was the significance of Jesus having communion with the disciples and Judas, the betrayer, being at the same table? (Refer to *Matthew 26:20-29.*)

3. How does one practically prepare to partake of communion?

4. What aspect of this lesson specifically spoke to you?

Memory Verse:

1 Corinthians 11:26

Church Discipline

Introduction

The truth of the Local Church functioning in a New Testament order is exciting. The Church being brought together in unity and harmony with the joyful presence of the Lord are true signs of a healthy Local Church. The Church is also a family, with God-given order, authority, privileges and responsibilities. In the family of God, there is also discipline of unruly or rebellious children; as in the natural, so in the spiritual. Church discipline is the corrective action that a Church body must take to insure the proper conduct or behavior of its members.

I. The Need for Church Discipline

A. The sin of one person has the power to affect the whole Church. *Jos 7:1-26*

B. The sin of one person, or party, has the power of leaven, which will in turn leaven the whole lump. *1 Cor 5:1-13; 2 Tm 2:16-18*

C. The concealment and practicing of sin in the Church will cause confusion and give the enemy opportunity to snare the young of the flock.

D. The lack of Church discipline where there is known sin will cause the unbelievers to mock the Church, and the Believers to become puffed up in their own deceit. *1 Cor 5:2*

II. The Biblical Perspective of Church Discipline

A. The Bible commands the leadership of the Local Church to:

1. _____ *2 Tm 4:2; Ti 2:15* (Greek, *"to convict, expose, correct, to show one his fault"*)

2. _____ *2 Tm 4:2; Ti 1:13* (Greek, *"to tax with a fault, chide, reprove"*)

3. _____ *1 Thes 5:12* (Greek, *"to admonish by warning, exhortation"*)

4. _____ *1 Cor 5:3, 12-13* (Gk, *"to separate or put asunder, to pro-nounce an opinion of right or wrong"*)

5. _____ *2 Tim 3:16* (Gk, *"to restore to an upright or right state, to raise up again, to reform"*)

6. _____ *Rom 16:17* (Gk, *"to regard, take heed"*)

B. The Bible commands the Church to discipline those who need it by:

1. _____ *2 Thes 3:6-14; 1 Tm 6:5*   (a disorderly person)

2. _____ *1 Tm 1:20*   (a blasphemer)

3. _____ *Ti 3:9-11*   (a heretic)

4. _____ *1 Cor 5:1-13*   (a fornicator,
a covetous person,
an idolater,
a railer,
a drunkard,
an extortioner)

5. _____ *Mt 18:15-18*   (a trespasser,
non-repentent)

Note: These Scriptures show that a spiritual membership did actually exist in the New Testament Local Churches. They could never have put out someone who was not joined to them, a part of the Body. People who are members of the universal, mystical and invisible church must be a member of a Local Church in order for this Scriptural pattern to be fulfilled.

III. The Purpose of Church Discipline

A. To keep the Church as the pillar and ground of righteousness and truth, an holy habitation of the Lord.

B. To protect the flock of God from the leaven of sin and to keep the Church a place of safety for all members of the family.

C. To bring the fear of the Lord into all the Church and an attitude of respect and honor toward the church.

D. To restore and bring repentance to the one who is being disciplined. *1 Cor 5:5; 2 Cor 2:4-11; Heb 12:9-12*

IV. The Spirit and Attitude of Those Who Discipline

A. The disciplining Church and leadership must be _____.

B. The disciplining Church and leadership must be _____.

C. The disciplining Church and leadership must be _____.

D. The disciplining Church and leadership must be _____.
   1 Thes 2:1-12; Ps 141:5; Prv 25:12

Questions:

1. How do we balance the ministry of mercy and discipline?

2. How long should a sinning member be given mercy and longsuffering before discipline is given?

3. Why is Church discipline so important?

4. What has this lesson caused you to feel?

Memory Verse:

1 Corinthians 5:6-7

Finding the Will of God

Introduction

This is an area of great interest to all Believers — everyone wants to find out what is the will of God. Much frustration and discouragement can come because of a lack of knowing how to discover what the will of God is for your life. In this lesson, we will define the will of God and present biblical basis for discovering and walking in the will of God.

I. Defining the Will of God

A. Two aspects of the will of God

  1. _____

   (a) *unconditional, immutable, irresistible*

   (b) *works all things after the counsel of His own will. Eph 1:11*

   (c) *according to the good pleasure of His will. Eph 1:9; God does things in a certain way because it pleases Him.*

   (d) *God's determined will encompasses such things as the birth of Christ, His death, resurrection, His ultimate triumph over sin, the judgment of Satan, etc.*

  2. _____

   (a) *the conscious and deliberate choice for which man is held responsible. Sometimes man is successful in living out God's will, and other times, he is not.*

   (b) *The will of God is that which God desires for our life, which can only be God's best. God's will is for the Believer to fulfill his potential.*

B. The Biblical words used to denote the Will of God.

  1. _____ — *2 Tm 1:9 "saved us according to His purpose"* (*Greek, to set before oneself, to purpose. God has set before us His goal and His purpose; this is the will of God.*)

2. _____ — *Eph 1:9* (Greek, *"that which seems good or pleasing to God, to be pleased with something, to think something good."*)

3. _____ — *Eph 1:9* (Greek, *"desire which stems from the heart, to desire something from the heart."*)

II. Problems with the Will of God

A. The term *"the will of God"* is sometimes not clearly defined or consistent.

B. Many are ignorant concerning the procedures one goes through to determine the will of God.

C. The term is frequently misused by some who try to justify some strange decision or action.

D. The term is used to defend doctrinal or conceptual views held by some.

E. The term is used as a magical formula to sanctify anything a person does.

F. There are many problems in applying general Biblical principles to specific life situation.

III. Biblical Promises Concerning Guidance

A. *Ps 25:9* — the meek will He guide.

B. *Ps 32:8* — I will guide thee with mine eye.

C. *Ps 73:24* — thou shalt guide me with thy counsel.

E. *Is 58:11* — and the Lord shall guide thee continually.

E. *Jer 3:4* — thou art the guide of my youth.

F. *Jn 16:13* — He will guide you into all truth.

G. *Mt 23:15* — woe unto you, you blind guides.

IV. Knowing the Will of God

A. The will of God is never _____ to the _____.
   Ps 119:1-11, 30-33

B. The will of God will never lead you to do something _____ to the

   _____ of God.

C. The will of God is not _____ from us — *Eph 1:9; 5:17; Col 1:9*

D. The will of God is something we _____, not just something we _____
_____ find. *1 Thes 5:16-21*

E. The will of God is _____ and _____ — *Eph 6:6*

F. The will of God is _____ and _____ — the specific
will of God can only be found as one is doing the general will of God.

G. The will of God is discovered when you let Jesus into every area of your life, which is
total _____.

H. The will of God can only be found when you are _____ to _____
_____ what the Lord has for your life.

V. Confirmations to the Will of God

A. The _____ in your life.

B. The _____ in your life.

C. The _____ over us in the Lord.

D. The _____ of God.

E. The _____ peace.

F. The _____ and _____ doors.

G. The _____ prophecies over you.

H. The _____ of your life.

I. The _____ and _____ given you to
do certain things.

Laying on of Hands/Prophecy

Introduction

In this lesson, the doctrine of the laying on of hands will be studied, with emphasis upon the Presbytery. This is another tremendous truth the Lord is restoring to the Church. There are many questions on this area that we hope to answer in this lesson.

I. The First Principles of the Doctrines of Christ

Hebrews 6:1-3

A. Repentance from dead works.

B. Faith toward God.

C. Doctrine of baptisms.

D. Laying on of hands.

E. Resurrection from the dead.

F. Eternal judgment.

II. The Doctrine of the Laying on of Hands

A. The importance of *"hands"*

In the Old Testament, they thought of the hands as an extension of the person himself. To give someone your hand meant to give yourself in commitment. To lay hands upon something was to transfer what you were to the thing on which you laid your hands. The hand is considered the extension of the person, his power to labor, his power to give, his power to fight. The hand lifted up in oath is important in creating a covenant. The hand speaks of identification, impartation, blessing and strength.

B. Laying on of hands in the Old Testament

1. To impart _____, _____, _____
   and _____. *Heb 11:20-21; Gn 48:14-16; Lv 9:22*

2. To ordain _____ to the _____. *Nm 8:5-22*

3. To _____ and _____ guilt. *Lv 1:4; 3:2; 4:15, 24, 29;*
   1 Tm 5:22

4. To impart _____ and _____ to young
   leadership. *Dt 34:9*

5. To _____ leadership to the ministry. *Nm 27:18-23*

C. Laying on of hands in the New Testament

1. To minister _____ to the sick. *Lk 4:40; 13:11-13; Mk 16:18; Acts 5:12*

2. To minister the _____ of the Holy Spirit. *Acts 9:17; 19:6-7*

3. To bless and _____ ministry. *Acts 13:1-4*

4. To _____, place and set leaders into their God-given ministry.
   Acts 6:1-6; Ti 1:5; 1 Tm 5:17-22

5. To impart _____. *1 Tm 4:14; 2 Tm 1:6; Rom 1:11*

6. To minister _____ and _____. *Acts 5:12; 14:3*

7. To _____ children. *Mt 19:15; Mk 10:16*

8. To _____ or _____ Believers in the faith, in
   their place of service in the House of the Lord. *Heb 6:2*

D. Illustration of the Doctrine of the Laying on of Hands

1. The boards in the Tabernacle of Moses. *Ex 26:1-37; 36:8-38*

2. The boards, the silver sockets, and the tenons that held them in place. *Ex 26:17*
   (Hebrew, *"tenons", hands*)

3. The purpose of the tenons, or hands, was to hold each board straight and steadfast and to have them set in divine order.

III. The Laying on of Hands and Presbytery

A. Two levels of the laying on of hands and ministry.

1. *The Local Church.* This occurs when the Local Church *eldership* (Presbytery) prays and ministers over those in the local body. This could involve any of the above-mentioned areas as found under letter *C.* The local ministers could also lay hands and minister the word of knowledge or prophecy. In our particular church, this could happen at any corporate church gathering when there is proper biblical oversight to judge the prophecy that is given. The local ministry could also lay hands on those who are becoming members of the church at the time of public presentation. This would be for *blessing* and *confirmation.* There may be times when prophecy would accompany the laying on of hands, but this would be only as the Spirit moved. The normal public laying on of hands for new members would normally be without any prophetic word.

2. Another scriptural usage of laying on of hands that is usually "accompanied with a prophetic word" and referred to in Scripture as a "Presbytery Meeting" is found in the following Scriptures:

   (a) 1 Tm 1:18

   (b) 1 Tm 4:14

   (c) 2 Tm 1:6

   (d) Acts 13:1-3

   (e) Nm 27:18-23

   (f) Gn 48:14

As we examine each of these Scriptures, it seems to be clear that the laying on of hands of the presbytery and the ordination of ministry flow together. All of these Scriptures reveal a level of ministry that seems to be only for those that are Apostles, Prophets, Evangelists, Pastors, Teachers being ordained as local elders or deacons and/or being sent out as missionaries.

This level of "Presbytery meeting" would include prayer and fasting as preparation on the part of the candidates and a planned meeting when there would be the laying on of hands and the prophetic word. The Presbyters in this level of Presbytery meeting would be Apostles and Prophets that would join with the pastoral ministry of the local church to minister the laying on of hands. The Apostles and prophets would be outside ministry invited in to specifically minister in this capacity. Let us state once again what would precipitate this level of Presbytery Meeting:

(a) *Ordaining of Elders*

(b) *Recognition and placement of Deacons*

(c) *Sending out of missionaries or missionary teams*

(d) *Ordaining and recognition of Five-Fold Ministry in the local church*

    (1) *Apostle*

    (2) *Prophet*

    (3) *Evangelist*

    (4) *Pastor*

    (5) *Teacher*

B. The Presbytery

1 Timothy 4:14

1. Presbytery:— Greek, *presbuterion* — *"a body of elders, council or senate of elders gathered together"*

Translated in *Luke 22:66* — the *elders* of the people
               Acts 22:5 — and all of the estate of the *elders*

Questions:

1. What can we expect when Godly men lay hands upon properly prepared people?

2. Explain in your own words the meaning of Presbytery, its purpose and benefits.

3. What part of this lesson especially ministered to you?

Memory Verse:

1 Timothy 4:14

Local Church Placement

Introduction

Is 2:3 "He will teach us His ways"
Is 55:6-10 "my ways are higher than your ways ..."

- The way the Lord builds a Church is higher and different than our ways.
- The way the Lord disciplines and deals with people is different than our ways.
- The way the Lord makes a servant or man of God is different than our ways.
- The way the Lord places and promotes people is different than our ways.

This is one reason many people are so confused, angry and bitter — they misunderstand the ways of the Lord — after they graduate from Bible College, what they expect is usually not what they get. God's way of placing and promoting ministries is obviously not man's way. We must embrace God's ways.

I. The Principle of Placement

Eph 4:15 — fitted together

A. We must be set into the Body or Local Church by God

Set:— Greek, *"to put or to place, to set or to establish, fit in a certain place"*

1. *1 Cor 12:18, 28 — "God set members in the Body as it hath pleased Him," "And God hath set some in the Church ..."*

   v. 18 (Amplified) "But as it is, God has placed and arranged the limbs and organs of the Body, each particular one of them just as He wished and saw fit and with the best adaptation."

2. *Ps 68:6 — "God setteth the solitary in families"*

3. *Prv 27:8 — "As a bird that wandereth from her nest, so is a man that wandereth from his place."*

B. We must accept God's placement — *Rom 12:1-8*

    1. *Rom 12:3-4 — "not to think of himself more highly than he ought to think; but to think soberly, according as God hath dealt to every man the measure of faith..."*

    (Amplified) *"For I warn every one among you not to estimate and think of himself more highly than he ought, not to have an exaggerated opinion of his own importance, but to rate his ability with sober judgment ..."*

    2. Soberly:— Greek, *"to be in a right mind, to exercise self-control, to put a moderate estimate upon one's self, to curb one's passion."*

II. The Principle of Promotion

Mk 10:35-45 — misunderstanding concerning placement and promotion

A. Definition of *"promotion"*

    1. To forward, advance, enlarge

    2. To exalt, elevate, raise, to be preferred in rank or honor, advancement

    3. To become lifted up, prospered

1 Tim 3:6 — "not a novice" (Greek, *"newly planted"*)
"lest being lifted up with pride, he fall"

B. Wrong concepts of promotion

    1. Because of my educational background, accomplishments, talents and abilities.

    2. Because of my age, seniority as in world business advancement, climbing the ladder to success.

    3. Because of what I do — I have many responsibilities; I use them as stepping stones to get to the place I want. (God sees the heart.)

janitor → *assistant teacher* → *teacher* → *assistant home leader* → *home leader* → *pastor!*

C. The law of promotion illustrated in the horn

    1. The horn in Scripture represents:
       • anointing
       • power

- fruitfulness
- the servant of the Lord and his ministry
- mouthpiece for the Lord

2. *1 Sm 2:1-10* — Hannah's horn (Samuel) was exalted

3. *Pss 89:17-24; 92:10; 132:17-18*

4. *Ps 75:4-5* — the righteous horns are exalted

5. *Lk 1:69; Phi 2:5-9* — the pattern horn (Jesus) exalted

D. Six Biblical causes of promotion

1. *Jgs 9:8-15* —promotion comes when you abide in the place God has set you.

2. *Gn 37-42* — promotion comes when you handle the dealings of God correctly, thus proving your attitudes under great testing.

3. *Mt 23:11-12* — promotion comes when you can rejoice in another person's advancement and serve them, even if they are less qualified than you.

4. *1 Pt 5:5-6* — promotion comes when humility has illed self-projection.

5. *Ps 75:10* — promotion comes when character is developed and proven stable.

6. *Dn 3:30* — promotion comes when faithfulness is shown toward all tasks, whether small or great, proving good stewardship.

II. The Problem of Self Ambition

Ambition:— Latin, *"to go about"*

English, *"an eager and sometimes inordinate desire for something, as preferment, honor superiority, power, fame wealth; to desire to promote oneself in some way"*

Greek, *"Originally meant a day laborer who worked for wages and had no motivation for service; canvassing for public office, not for service they could render the state, but solely for their own honor, glory and profit"*

Translation in the New Testament:

1. *Rom 2:8* — contentious
2. *2 Cor 12:20* — strife and Church problems
3. *Gal 4:20* — strife, works of the flesh
4. *Phil 1:16* — contentions, wrong motives for preaching
5. *Jas 3:14* — strife, wisdom that is not from above
6. *Phil 2:3* — strife, wrong spirit in which to live
7. *Jas 3:16* — strife

IV. The Effects of Self Ambition

A. Self ambition brings *destruction* — *Prv 17:19*

B. Self ambition brings *shame* — *Prv 3:35*

C. Self ambition brings *deception* — *Ob 3-5*

D. Self ambition cause the Body of Christ to come to ruins — *2 Cor 12:20; 11:26; Gal 5:20*

E. Self ambition brings a servant down to *abasement* — *2 Cor 10:5; Ez 21:26; Lk 14:11; 18:14*

STUDY NOTES:

Additional resources available through

CityChristianPublishing
www.CityChristianPublishing.com

Leadership

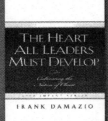

Church Growth

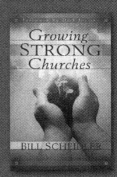

Life Impact

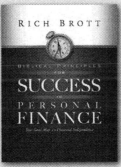

Finance/ Business

City Christian Publishing, 9200 NE Fremont St, Portland, OR 97220
Call: 1-800-777-6057 Fax: 1-503-257-2228 **Visit us:** www.CityChristianPublishing.com

CPSIA information can be obtained
at www.ICGtesting.com
Printed in the USA
LVOW06s0002150917

548684LV00038B/921/P